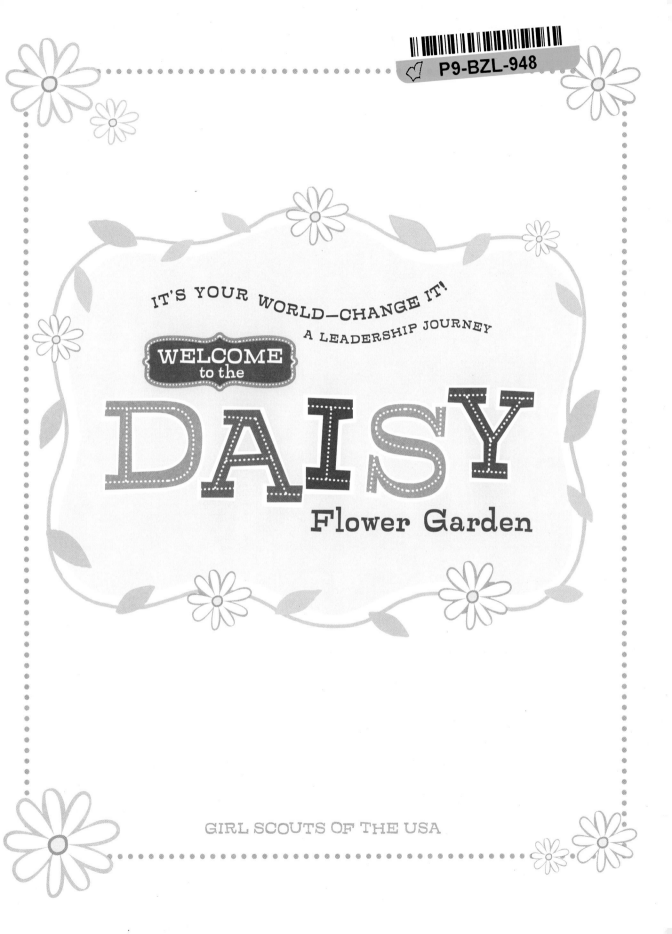

IT'S YOUR WORLD—CHANGE IT!

A LEADERSHIP JOURNEY

WELCOME to the

DAISY

Flower Garden

GIRL SCOUTS OF THE USA

Chair, National Board of Directors	Chief Executive Officer	Vice President, Girl Experience
Kathy Hopinkah Hannan	**Sylvia Acevedo**	**Jennifer Allebach**

Senior Director, Program Resources:
Suzanne Harper
Art Director: Douglas Bantz
Writer: Laura J. Tuchman
Contributors: Editorial Services, FableVision
Illustrator: Jennifer Kalis
Designer: Parham Santana

© 2008 by Girl Scouts of the USA

First published in 2008 by Girl Scouts of the USA
420 Fifth Avenue, New York, NY 10018-2798
www.girlscouts.org

ISBN: 978-0-88441-709-5

All rights reserved. Except for pages intended for reuse by Girl Scout volunteers, this book may not be reproduced in whole or in part in any form or by any means, electronic or mechanical, including photocopying, recording, or by any information storage or retrieval system now known or hereafter invented, without the prior written permission of Girl Scouts of the United States of America.

Printed in Canada

11 12 13/21 20 19

Page 60: Jef Meul/Foto Natura/Minden Pictures/
Getty Images

The women mentioned in this book are examples of how women have used their voice in the world. This doesn't mean that GSUSA (or you) will agree with everything they have ever done or said.

MIX
Paper from
responsible sources
FSC® C011825

Welcome to the Daisy Flower Garden

Congratulations!
You're a Girl Scout Daisy.

You are starting a big adventure. In Girl Scouts, we call it a journey.
You and your sister Girl Scouts are going to the Daisy Flower Garden.
It's an amazing place filled with flowers of all colors and shapes and sizes.
Here's a song to get you started:

I'm a Girl Scout Daisy! Take a look at me.

I'm a Girl Scout Daisy, happy as can be.

I'm going on a journey,

With friends along the way,

I'm a Girl Scout Daisy,

Hip, Hip, Hurray!

In the Daisy Garden, you'll meet lots of friends. Some will be Girl Scout
Daisies just like you. Some will be flowers—beautiful flowers from all over
the world. And some will be critters—buzzing bees, lovely ladybugs, wiggly
worms. All these friends have wonderful things to show you.

But before you go to the garden, let's meet the very first Girl Scout Daisy.

The First Girl Scout Daisy

The first Daisy was Juliette Gordon Low. Her family called her Daisy. When Daisy was a girl, she loved to climb trees. She even liked to swing on vines. As Daisy grew older, she wanted girls to have as much fun as she did. She wanted them to grow up and be whatever they wanted in life. That's why she started Girl Scouts.

The first Girl Scouts were from Savannah, Georgia. Now there are Girl Scouts all over the world.

And here you are, a Girl Scout Daisy ready to enter the Daisy Flower Garden. Let's meet the three girls who will take you there.

The Garden Girls

Cora, Campbell, and Chandra are Best Friends
Forever, or BFFs. They are all Girl Scout Daisies.
They are 7 years old and finishing the first grade.

COLOR ME!

Chandra lives with her mother and father and grandma near an old garden. Everyone in Chandra's family was born in India. India is a big country with many, many people.

More than anything, Chandra loves to sit in the kitchen and watch her grandma cook. Sometimes Chandra's little orange cat, Pumpkin, watches, too. One of Chandra's favorite foods is samosas. Samosas are like little fried pies, but not sweet. Chandra's favorite samosas are filled with potatoes and peas.

Chandra also likes to draw and paint and learn about the moon and the stars. In a very old language of India, Chandra's name means "moon."

All About Me!

I like to _____ and _____ .

My favorite animal is _____ .

Here's what it looks like:

Bonus Question

Let a family member or friend help you answer this:

My name means

_____ .

COLOR ME!

Cora lives with her parents and two older brothers. Her parents are from Mexico. Her great-great-grandparents were born in Spain. Some day, Cora hopes to visit Spain.

Cora loves music, and she loves to make her friends laugh. When Cora walks, she likes to swing her head from side to side so her hair swings from side to side, too. Her full name is Corazón. Corazón means "heart" in Spanish.

Cora's brothers call her Cori because she loves the leaves of the coriander plant, which is an herb. Those leaves look like parsley, but they're called cilantro. Cora's dad chops them up and puts them in guacamole. That's Cora's favorite snack.

Me and My Family!

I live with _____ . Here's a picture of my family:

My family calls me _____ .

My family's favorite snack is _____ .

Plants Help People!

Cora has never had a tummy ache. Do you know why? Because she eats cilantro! Cilantro is so powerful, it can calm an upset tummy. What other herbs are good for you? Have a family member or friend help you discover the answer.

What is the Most Popular Herb in the World?

People all around the world eat cilantro. And they eat a lot of cilantro—more than all other herbs put together.

COLOR ME!

Campbell lives with her mom and little sister, Sage. She loves sports. She is happiest outdoors, riding her skateboard. Campbell and her family used to live in Georgia. Her great-grandparents came to America from Ireland and Italy.

Campbell loves learning Spanish words from her friend Cora. Here's a list of some new words she has learned:

hi = *hola*

bye = *adiós*

flowers = *flores*

trees = *árboles*

sun = *sol*

water = *agua*

friend = *amiga*

tomato = *tomate*

Me and My World!

When I'm outside, I like to _____ .
Draw a picture of it!

My favorite place is _____ . This is what it looks like:

Some day, I want to visit _____ .

What's a Promise?

The Girl Scout Promise is the way Girl Scouts promise to act every day. By the time you are ready to be a Girl Scout Brownie, you will know the Girl Scout Promise by heart.

The Girl Scout Promise

On my honor, I will try:

To serve God and my country,

To help people at all times,

And to live by the Girl Scout Law.

Now that you know what the Promise is all about, let's go to the Daisy Flower Garden.

Garden
Hours
a.m. to 5p.m.
ONLY

Amazing Daisy and the Daisy Flower Garden

Chapter 1
One Little Daisy Shining in the Sun

Cora, Chandra, and Campbell were not having the best day. It all started when Anika brought her grandmother's ring for show-and-tell. It was silver and sparkly and had a bright-red ruby. Suddenly, the green-and-purple scarf Cora's grandmother knit for her didn't seem so cool.

Then, at recess, Campbell played second base in softball. As usual, she caught every ball, high or low, that came her way. Marco, the shortstop, didn't catch anything. He yelled at Campbell: "Stop hogging the ball!" Campbell wasn't happy.

Later, in reading class, Chandra raised her hand to read one of the funny rhymes in their reading book. The teacher never called on her.

The girls were quiet as they walked home together.

They passed the old community garden. As usual, it was full of weeds. On the garden gate was a big black sign that read:

"Garden hours 9 a.m. to 5 p.m. ONLY."

Chandra stopped. She saw something bright flash among the tall weeds inside the garden gate. It was a single white daisy.

"Look!" cried Chandra as she ran through the open gate. Cora and Campbell ran right behind her. "Look at this little daisy, happy as can be in this messy place."

They all watched the daisy as it swayed in the cool breeze.

"I wish this garden had hundreds of happy flowers like this one," Campbell said.

WORDS FOR THE WISE!

Plop, plop, plop! Plop means to drop.

You can plop yourself down, right on the ground.

When something goes plop,

it sounds like it dropped . . . into water.

Raindrops go plop. Plop, plop, plop.

A lot of raindrop plops make a puddle.

Jump in the puddle to make one big

. . . . !

"That would take a lot of work," said Cora. "We couldn't do it by ourselves."

"Well, maybe some day," Chandra said. "Let's sit and rest a while." She spread her jacket on the scrubby grass beside the daisy and **plopped** down. Then she pulled out a bag of delicious little samosas filled with potatoes and peas.

The girls sat beside the daisy and ate and talked. One by one, they stretched out in the sun with their backpacks under their heads. Soon they were sound asleep.

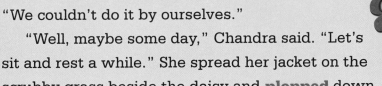

Getting to Know
Girl Scout Stuff

Girl Scouting connects you to Girl Scouts all around the world, and to all the girls who were Girl Scouts before you. All Girl Scouts share some special things:

The Girl Scout Sign

 The Girl Scout sign is something Girl Scouts make when they say the Girl Scout Promise. The three straight fingers stand for the three parts of the Promise.

Girl Scout Handshake

 Girl Scouts greet each other with the Girl Scout handshake. They shake their left hands and make the Girl Scout Sign with their right hand. Do you know why?

Friendship Circle

 The Friendship Circle is a way to end Girl Scout meetings. Everyone gathers in a circle and crosses her right arm over her left and holds hands with the girls on either side. While in a Friendship Circle, Girl Scouts often do a friendship squeeze. Can you guess what that is?

Sing a Girl Scout Daisy Song

Here's a song for Girl Scout Daisies. Chant it or sing it any way you like. It was written by a Girl Scout named Sandy. Sandy travels all over the world and meets Girl Scout Daisies wherever she goes.

Sandy's Song
for Girl Scout Daisies

I'm a Girl Scout Daisy! Take a look at me.

I'm a Girl Scout Daisy, happy as can be.

We're having fun and sharing,

Each and every day.

I'm a Girl Scout Daisy,

Hip, Hip, Hurray!

Chapter 2
A Smiling Bee and a Special Key

"Oh, no! It's after 5. We fell asleep. We're in *big* trouble," Chandra cried. She jumped up and grabbed her backpack. "The garden gate locked at 5 o'clock. What are we going to do?"

Cora rubbed her eyes. "Don't worry. Someone will help us."

In a flash, a small, golden bee landed right on top of Campbell's head. Campbell froze, and Chandra began to tiptoe toward her to swat the bee away. But just as Chandra reached out her hand, the bee buzzed straight toward Chandra's head.

Now Campbell started to reach over to swat the bee away, when—*bzzz . . . zzzz.* The bee flew up and over to Cora. It buzzed right in front of her face. Then it turned and flew over to a big red maple tree. Then the bee turned *again,* and flew back to Cora.

The girls watched as the bee buzzed back and forth from Cora to the tree, as if doing a little dance.

Cora looked at her friends. "I know this sounds *loco.* You know, really *crazy.* But I think that bee is trying to tell us something. Let's see what's under that tree."

The girls walked to the tree, *and* the bee buzzed right alongside them. *Bzzz . . . zzzz.* Suddenly, the bee swooped and touched Chandra's hand. Then it swooped again, touching the ground under the tree.

"Maybe we should dig under this tree," Chandra said. She grabbed a small broken branch and began to dig right where the bee landed. Cora and Campbell grabbed fallen branches and joined her. Suddenly, the girls heard a *clink.* Chandra's branch hit something hard. Digging faster and faster, the girls uncovered a small tin box. The box was covered with rust. It looked like it had been in the dirt a long, long time.

"This could be a secret treasure," Campbell said with glee.

What Did That Bee Say?

Honeybees talk to each other. They just don't use words. To tell each other where food is, they dance in the air.

Draw It!

If you were digging in a garden, what would you like to find?

The girls plopped down under the tree. They turned the box over and over. Each time they turned the box, they heard a small sound. It seemed that whatever was inside was light or soft. Working together, the girls opened the rusted latch. The hinges gave a loud creak and threw off bits of rusty paint. Chandra turned the box upside down. Out fell a tightly folded piece of paper. The paper was yellow, instead of white.

"This looks very old," Chandra said. She unfolded the paper and out fell a tiny green key.

"A key! I knew it. A key to a secret treasure," Campbell shouted.

"What does the note say? Who is it from?" Cora and Campbell shouted together.

"It says, *'This is a message from Daisy Gordon Low,'*" Chandra read excitedly. "It says she put this note here with the first Girl Scouts in 1912. They were from Savannah, Georgia. That means this box is really old—older than our parents. And older than my grandma!"

"And from Georgia, where I'm from," said Campbell. "But I've never been to Savannah."

Campbell grabbed the note from Chandra and began to read aloud, *"'You are sitting in a special place.'"* Campbell looked up at her friends.

"Special? This old garden?" said Cora.

"That's what it says!" Campbell began to read again.

This garden is a wonderful place. My Girl Scouts enjoyed this garden for a whole year. Now that you have found our message, the garden is yours to enjoy. But it is also a big responsibility. It needs a lot of care.

In this note is the key to the garden gate. It is just a small key. You will have many more important keys as you grow older. But as long as you hold on to this little key and keep it safe, the garden gate will always open for you. And I promise you that the more you visit the garden, the more you will get in return.

The girls looked at the little green key and the small tin box. "This seems like an important message," said Cora. "We better think about it and read it again before we tell anyone else about it."

Then Cora jumped up. "*¡Vámonos!* Let's go," she shouted. "We have to get home."

Chandra carefully placed the note back in the tin box and put the box in her backpack. She handed the key to Cora.

Then the girls raced to the garden gate. Just as Cora was about to put the key in the gate's rusty old lock, the gate swung open. Just like that. Suddenly, the girls heard a buzz in the air. *Bzzz . . . zzzz.* Cora, Campbell, and Chandra looked up and saw the little golden bee fly by. "This might sound *crazy,*" Campbell said slowly, "but I think that bee just smiled at us."

All About Keys!

My family has _____ keys.

Our keys unlock _____ .

_____ .

_____ .

_____ .

Someday, I want a key to _____ .

_____ .

_____ .

_____ .

_____ .

Chapter 3
Amazing Daisy and Her Flower Family

T he next day at school, Cora, Campbell, and Chandra could not contain their excitement. They wanted to care for the garden, but they didn't know how. They huddled at lunch and talked. At recess, they talked some more. Finally, they decided what to do. They would clean up the weeds around that smiling white daisy. That would be a good start.

As soon as school let out, they raced to the garden. They ran right through the garden gate. But what a surprise! The old, weedy garden was . . . gone!

Instead, **mounds** and **mounds** of flowers waved in front of them. These new flowers all looked a little like that first happy daisy. But they were different, too. And they were in every color of the rainbow.

The girls looked around. They didn't know what to think. Suddenly, they saw the little golden bee buzzing toward them.

"The bee," whispered Chandra.

But Cora and Campbell didn't hear Chandra. They were down on their hands and knees, looking at the flowers. Cora looked up at Chandra. "This flower has eyes, Chandra."

WORDS FOR THE WISE!

What is a mound? A mound is a pile. A mound could weigh a pound. But a mound of flowers would be much lighter than a pound of flour.

"What do you mean? Flowers don't have eyes."
Campbell stood up quickly. "Yes, it does. It has eyes.
And . . . and . . ."

"A mouth, too!" Cora and Campbell said
together.

Chandra got down on her knees to look at the
little white daisy, the same daisy she had first seen
through the garden gate. She looked right in the
middle of the daisy's white petals. What she saw
made her laugh.

A happy, smiling yellow face was peeking out from those beautiful white petals. And instead of just green leaves on her flower stem, this daisy had tiny, leafy arms poking out. The daisy smiled and waved at Chandra.

"Hi," the daisy said in her small daisy voice.

"Did you just say, 'Hi?'" asked Chandra.

"Yes. Hi," said the daisy. "My name is Amazing Daisy."

Cora and Campbell sat down next to Chandra.

"You *are* amazing," said Cora.

"Not really," Daisy said with a laugh. *"You* are the ones who brought me to life, just like Daisy Gordon Low did so many years ago! I'm so sorry I didn't say hello on your last visit. I always try to be friendly, but it was *sooo* late in the day. I'm a daisy, you know, so I close my petals when the sun starts to go down. I need to get to bed early and get my rest. But I know you met Honey, my buzzing bee friend. I'll tell you more about her later. First, come meet my three favorite cousins."

All About Daisies!

A daisy is really hundreds of tiny flowers surrounded by big petals. Those petals are called rays. Daisies like a lot of sun, and they're very strong. Just like Amazing Daisy, real daisies can get by with very little attention. And they *really do* close their petals at night.

Daisy waved her little leafy hand, and three flowers swayed over to her. One of them was tall and important-looking.

"This is Sunny, the sunflower," Daisy said. "She's my cousin from Great Britain. She's always friendly and helpful."

"How do you do?" Sunny, the sunflower, said.

"There's Zinni, too. She's the most considerate and caring friend I have," Daisy said. "She's my cousin from Mexico."

"Mexico! That's where my family is from," said Cora.

The spring-green flower smiled and waved. "My full name is Zinnia, but I like to be called Zinni," she said.

"And Mari, the marigold—she's a cousin, too. She's from Africa and has family in France, Central America, *and* Mexico. She's older and very responsible. She's especially good at keeping bugs out of our garden." The bright-orange flower bowed and said hello.

Amazing Daisy turned to her three cousins and pointed to the girls. "Meet Chandra, Cora, and Campbell."

Daisies, Daisies Everywhere!

Daisies are part of the largest flower family in the world. Sunflowers, zinnias, dahlias, chrysanthemums, marigolds, and asters are all in the same flower family.

Daisy

Sunflower

Zinnia

Dahlia

Chrysanthemum

Marigold

Aster

"It is so nice to meet you," said Mari. "We are a very big family—the Daisy family. We have aunts and uncles and cousins all over the world, even as far away as China and Japan. But we haven't talked with little girls in a long time."

"That's why Daisy Gordon Low was so special to us," said Daisy. "She knew so many Girl Scouts. She believed in having friends all over the world. "Girl Scouting," she used to say, "can be the magic thread that links the youth of the world together."

"And our Daisy family is like a magic thread that links the flowers of the world," added Mari.

Suddenly, Zinni perked up. "Speaking of flowers of the world, we really miss all the flower friends we knew when Daisy Gordon Low was around. We have photos of all of them. I so miss Gloria, the morning glory. She always woke up first every morning. And she made the best blueberry pancakes."

"Well, our little garden world would certainly be better if we could see all our flower friends again," Daisy said. And then, Daisy's petals started to fold together, as if she were yawning. "My goodness, I guess it's time for me to go to sleep."

"It *is* late," said Cora. "We should get home."

Campbell sighed. "Darn. I wish we could stay."

The girls waved at the flowers. And the flowers all waved back.

"Bye," the girls said. "We'll come back tomorrow. Maybe we can help you find your flower friends again."

The girls walked slowly out of the garden. They were all thinking that tomorrow couldn't come soon enough.

How Does Your Garden Grow?

How is your mini-garden growing? What does it look like? Draw it!

What do you think it will be when it grows even more? Draw it!

Chapter 4
Flower Friends, Flower Needs

The morning dawned bright and sunny. The girls agreed to meet at the garden at 9 o'clock sharp. Chandra got there first, then Campbell, then Cora. They barely said hello before pushing open the big gate. But after just one step into the garden, their mouths fell open.

The beautiful garden they left behind the day before was now so much bigger and more beautiful. Green grass had sprung up all around. And there was clover, lots of clover. And there were so many more flowers: tulips, roses, violets, geraniums. And many more that the girls didn't even know the names of. They were *so* fancy-looking.

chirp

chirp

The girls looked around
in wonder. The air smelled so
sweet. Butterflies flitted about. Birds
chirped. A caterpillar wriggled. And the little
golden bee buzzed. A birdbath stood at the far edge of
the garden. Beyond that was a little pond. This was the most
beautiful garden the girls had ever seen.

chirp

chirp

"Good morning," called out Amazing Daisy. The girls turned to find Daisy swaying in the breeze, looking brighter than ever. "I don't know how you girls did it. All our flower friends showed up overnight," Daisy said.

"I *thought* about you and your friends before I fell asleep," said Chandra.

"I *dreamed* about you and your friends," said Campbell.

"I woke up *thinking* about you and your friends," said Cora.

"But we didn't *do* anything," all three girls cried out all at once.

"Well, good thoughts and good dreams are powerful indeed," Amazing Daisy sang out. "Now, come meet *all* my friends."

chirp

Lupe

Lupe, the lupine, is light blue. Her name is pronounced Loo-PAY. She's always cool and relaxed. And she's honest and fair. She was born in Texas and then moved to Minnesota. She spends her summers in Maine. She has family all around the world.

TuLa

Tula, the tulip, is red. She's courageous and strong. She's from the Netherlands. Her family moved there a long time ago from a land called Iran.

Gloria

Gerri

Gloria, the morning glory, is purple. She's all about respect. She respects herself and others. She's from California and has family throughout South America and Asia.

Gerri, the geranium, is magenta. That's a kind of red—a purplish red. Gerri is about respect, too. She always respects authority. She grew up in the mountains of Virginia and has family all around the world, especially in Greece.

Then Daisy pointed to the ground. "And this is Clover," she said. "She gives our garden a nice green carpet and white flowers, too. In fact, she gives lots of things to our garden: food for animals and bugs, good-luck charms for people, and sweet nectar. Her nectar helps our pal Honey make delicious clover honey. As Daisy Gordon Low used to say, 'Clover really knows how to use resources wisely.'"

Next, a delicate violet-colored flower stepped forward. "Hi, I'm Vi, the violet," the flower said. "I'm from Australia and I'm so thrilled to meet you. I hear you are Girl Scouts. I love being a sister to every Girl Scout."

Then, a beautiful, tall rose stepped forward. "And last, but certainly not least, here's Rosie, the rose," said Daisy. "As usual, she's trying to make the world a better place."

Rosie smiled at Daisy and the girls and shook their hands, one by one. "As you know," Rosie said, "we could all use a better world. I'm hoping you will all join me in making the world a better place. How about we start with this garden?"

"What could this beautiful garden possibly need?" Chandra wondered out loud.

"Oh, you'd be surprised how much a garden needs," Rosie said with a laugh.

"Yes, Rosie is right," said Lupe, "We need a lot of things to keep this garden growing. Let's think about this right now. We must all say what we *really* mean, for that's being *honest.* And we must be *fair.* We'll give each flower a turn to speak."

Lupe then turned to Daisy. "Daisy, you know each of us so well. Why don't you lead the group?"

"I'd be happy to," Daisy said. "Gerri, let's start with you."

Really Old Roses

Roses are native Americans. They've been growing in America for at least 35 million years. Roses grow in all 50 states. Our first president, George Washington, grew roses. So did our third president, Thomas Jefferson.

Jumpin' Geraniums

Geraniums grow in all sorts of places, all the way from Alaska to the tip of South America and beyond. Their sweet-smelling cousins are called scented geraniums. They come from South Africa and smell like lots of good things: lemon, rose, apple, peppermint, and more.

Gerri, the geranium, flashed her black eyes. "Well, you know," she said slowly, "I so miss my cousins from South Africa. *They* smell so good, and *I* barely have a scent. What I wouldn't give for a whiff of lavender, or the sweet smell of basil."

"Basil? I love basil," said Campbell. "I love to eat basil with tomatoes. I could plant some basil for you. Maybe some sage, too. My little sister is named Sage. She would love to smell real sage in this garden. She's almost 4. In another year, she'll be old enough to be a Girl Scout Daisy."

"Well, we would love to meet little Sage—another sister for us," Vi, the violet, said.

"And some **fragrant** friends will really make our world better," said Rose. "Sometimes even I get tired of smelling my sweet self."

Everyone laughed—all the flowers and all the girls.

Then Zinni stepped forward. "With all these new friends arriving, we're going to need some *really* good dirt . . . I mean *really* good soil," she added. "So I think we need more worms in this garden."

"Oh, Zinni," said Daisy, "thanks so much for thinking of our soil. You are so considerate and caring. We definitely need good soil to eat and grow."

WORDS FOR THE WISE!

Fragrant means to smell sweet or pleasant. Scented geraniums smell sweet and pleasant. What is your favorite smell?

"What do worms have to do with good soil?" Campbell asked.

"Oh, just about everything," said Zinni. "They wiggle all through it and keep it fresh."

"Hmm," said Campbell. "I thought worms were just little wiggly things that came out after the rain and hid under the doormat."

"Yes, worms are good, for sure. But if it's not too much to ask, I want some more honeybees," said Clover. "Not just for my little clover flowers, but to give Honey, our bee, some new friends, too."

"I'm afraid of having more bees in the garden," said Gerri. "That means more stingers. But, Clover, I also know that you know what you're talking about. You are the *authority* on bees. So I'll respect your wishes."

"And don't be afraid," chimed in Tula. "I have enough courage and strength for all of us. I'll lend you some."

"And I can help you, too," said Sunny. "I am so tall that I can see the bees buzzing all around the garden. I will let you know when I see a bee buzzing toward you."

"Thank you, Sunny," said Gerri. "You are always so friendly and helpful."

Sweet Stuff!

Did you know that bees have to visit about 2 million flowers just to make one jar of honey?

Lovely Ladybugs

Not all ladybugs are red and black. Some are yellow with black spots. Some are black with yellow or orange spots. Some are orange with white spots. And some have no spots at all.

"I'm more worried about bugs than bees," said Lupe. "How about some pretty ladybugs to keep the ugly bugs away?"

"Ugly bugs? You mean bugs that are bad for plants, like those little green bugs that stick to tomato plants?" Campbell asked.

"Yes, exactly," answered Lupe. "Those little green bugs are called aphids—A-P-H-I-D-S. Sometimes they really do a number on me."

"Wow, you flowers have a lot of needs," said Chandra. "I guess it takes a lot to keep a garden growing strong."

"Well, I know that growing basil is easy," said Campbell. "But we're going to have to think about how to get worms and bees . . ."

". . . and ladybugs," chimed in Chandra. "After all, we're just little girls."

"Well, you all seem quite big and powerful to me," said Rosie. "I'm sure you three can come up with a good plan."

"Maybe we can," said Cora. "Maybe we just need some time. Let's go. ¡Vámonos! Let's think about this over lunch. I'm hungry."

The Path to My Best Garden

Gardens need sun, water, and good care. To take care of your plants, you might even *talk* to them. Look at the garden path below—it needs help. Fill in the garden signs with your own rules for a great garden.

What's in Your Garden?

Do you know a garden near where you live? What makes it special?

Look at all the flowers and plants and critters and birds pictured here. If you could have your own garden, what would be in it? Make a picture of your garden. Use anything you like to "grow" your garden: crayons, pens, watercolor pencils, pictures, photos, stickers, dried flowers, dried leaves. All that matters is that your garden is special to *you*.

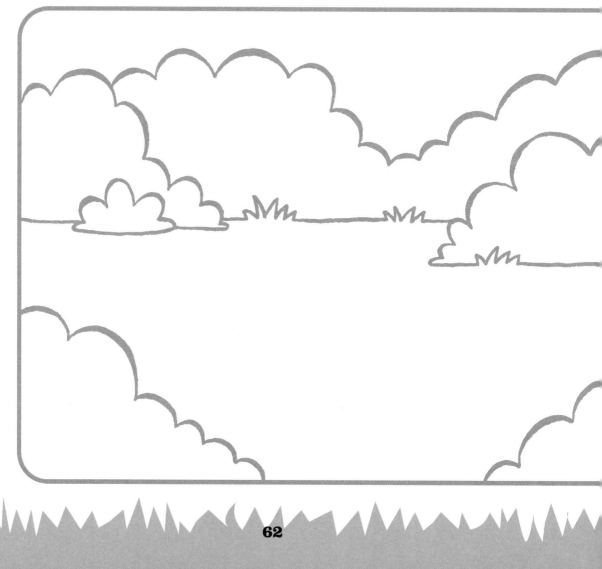

Living
the Girl Scout Law

The Girl Scout Law shows how Girl Scouts try to act toward one another and the world. Each of Amazing Daisy's flower friends tries her best to live one part of the Law. See if you can match the flowers to their parts of the Law.

Girl Scout Law

I will do my best to be

honest and fair,

friendly and helpful,

considerate and caring,

courageous and strong, and

responsible for what I say and do,

and to

respect myself and others,

respect authority,

use resources wisely,

make the world a better place, and

be a sister to every Girl Scout.

Sunny, the sunflower

Zinni, the zinnia

Mari, the marigold

Lupe, the lupine

Tula, the tulip

Gloria, the morning glory

Gerri, the geranium

Clover, the clover

Vi, the violet

Rosie, the rose

Flowers Live
the Girl Scout Law

Which flower do you want to be like? What would you do to be like that flower? Draw it.

Chapter 5
Tamales, Tomatoes, and Worm Talk, Too

The girls raced to Cora's house. Cora's father had his famous guacamole waiting for them. It was chunks of avocado with little pieces of tomato and red onion and cilantro. And there were crisp tortilla chips to go with it. Then came tamales made by Cora's grandma. These were little packets of soft corn dough filled with chicken.

Cora's mother poured each girl a cold rice drink. It was milky-looking and tasted of lime and cinnamon. "This is called *horchata*," Cora said.

Some Tongue Twister Fun!

Try saying this tongue twister really fast.

Cora chops coriander

to cheer her chum Chandra

and charm the chinchilla

who chitchats like a chatterbox

while chomping on chocolate.

The girls ate and drank. And they talked about the beautiful flowers and all their needs. Cora's mother listened in.

"The flowers asked you for worms? Those flowers have been asleep a long time," Cora's mother said with a laugh. "They don't just need worms. They need *worm composting*. You girls can help with that."

"Worm *what*?" Campbell asked.

"Worm composting," repeated Cora's mom. "It's a really neat way to make good soil for a garden. It's also a great way to recycle. You know how we put all our bottles and cans and newspapers in those special bins, right? That's recycling. Well, worms recycle, too. They recycle food scraps by eating them up. In fact, feeding worms food scraps is the easiest way to recycle that I can think of."

68

All three girls looked at Cora's mom. They wanted to know more.

"But, Mom," said Cora, "when we recycle bottles and cans and newspapers, a big truck stops by and collects them. Is someone going to collect our worms?"

"No, sweetie, you *keep* your worms. Worms eat up food scraps and turn out worm *castings.* That's a polite word for worm poop. That poop is very good for gardens."

"How come we never heard any of this before?" Cora asked.

Good-bye, Smelly Garbage

If every home had a worm composting box, there would be no food scraps to throw out. The days of smelly garbage would be over.

From Worms to Wonderful

Worm's are a gardener's best friend. They make black, spongy stuff that's really good for the soil. It looks like bunches of tiny, black, stuck-together balls. Just mix those little balls with potting soil and sand, and you get perfect plant soil.

"Well, good gardening tips are sometimes hard to come by," Cora's mother replied. "But a lady named Mary did her best to teach people about worm composting. In fact, she is probably as famous for worm composting as Daisy Gordon Low is for Girl Scouts. People called her Worm Woman. She lived in Kalamazoo, in Michigan.

"I can show you girls how to make a worm composting box," Cora's mom added. "You can keep it in the kitchen. And then every week, you can take fresh compost to the garden."

"I don't know," said Chandra, looking glum. "I don't think my mom will let me keep worm poop in our kitchen. That sounds yucky!"

"Well, the worms stay right in their box. It's all very neat and clean. But as long as the weather's mild, you can keep the box in your backyard . . . or in the garage or the basement."

"Still," Chandra said, "wouldn't it be more fun to grow ladybugs? They're so pretty."

"Gardens are about choices, Chandra," Cora's mother said. "Every gardener chooses what she wants to grow."

Worms Like to Be Comfy!

Worms like mild weather, 59 to 77 degrees.

"Basil," said Campbell, "that's what I want to grow—for Gerri and Rosie. They want to have more good smells in the garden."

"Basil is perfect then," Cora's mother said. "And maybe, since you love tomatoes, you'll plant those, too. I can give you seeds for some beautiful **heirloom** tomatoes from Mexico."

What Do Worms Eat?

Worms like vegetable and fruit scraps best. They will even eat banana peels.

Rainbow of Tomatoes!

Tomatoes grow in all colors—green, yellow, orange, pink. Mexico has a lot of pink tomatoes. Some people say tomatoes came from that country.

"Air loom?" asked Chandra. "What's an air loom? A loom that floats in the air?"

"No, silly, H-E-I-R-L-O-O-M," said Campbell. "That means old and special. I learned that from my grandma. She's always talking to me about heirlooms. But not tomatoes. She talks about heirloom jewelry. She's said she's going to give me her heirloom charm bracelet when I turn 8 next year."

"That must be a beautiful bracelet," Cora's mom said. "And heirloom tomatoes are beautiful, too. And delicious."

WORDS FOR THE WISE! ???

Sometimes words look and sound alike. Sometimes they don't. Heirloom starts with an H. But it sounds like it starts with an A!

"What about honeybees?" asked Cora. "Clover wants her bee friend, Honey, to have some more bees to play with."

"Honeybees? Hmm, that's a tough one," said Cora's mom. "Bees aren't doing so well this year. But I know all the beekeepers in town. Maybe you could visit a beekeeper and get some advice."

Suddenly, Cora remembered the note from Daisy Gordon Low. "Chandra, show my mom the note," she said.

Chandra pulled the rusty tin box from her backpack. She opened the box and took out the folded yellow note. She carefully unfolded the paper and handed it to Cora's mother.

Cora's mom sat down at the kitchen table and read the note. Then she looked up at the girls. "This is a wonderful note. That Daisy was very smart. Maybe you could write a note, too—to future Girl Scout Daisies. What would you want to tell them?"

"We have no *idea*," Cora, Chandra, and Campbell cried out all at once.

"Well, think about it a while. I'm sure the right message will come to you."

"Let's ask Tamiko," said Cora. "She's good at giving advice. She's almost 9 years old."

"Oh, Cora, I almost forgot," Cora's mother said. "Tamiko called this morning while you were at the garden. I told her to stop by around 1 o'clock, which is—" Cora's mother looked up at the big yellow kitchen clock—"right about now."

Just then the doorbell rang. It was Tamiko, a third-grader from down the street. She held a tray of beautiful little Japanese rice cakes. Some were pink. Some were green. Some were white.

Tamiko said hello to everyone and then set down the tray of cakes. "My mother sent these over for all of you to try," Tamiko said.

"Delicious!" said Cora's mom.

"Mmm, these *are* good," said Campbell. "Maybe when we finish helping the flowers, we could celebrate with a garden party. We could serve these cakes with tea. Garden parties are supposed to have tea, right?"

"What a great idea," said Cora. "We could start with guacamole and little tomato and basil sandwiches."

"Maybe rolled up like pinwheels so they're nice and pretty," said Chandra. "And we could have mint tea and these pretty cakes."

"Now that sounds like a *perfect* party," Tamiko said.

And everyone agreed.

Plant, Water, Grow!

What Our Garden Journey Project Was All About

Our Girl Scout Daisy group decided to

. . . .

I did my part by

. . . .

. . . .

I liked

. . . .

. . . .

. . . .

Time for Garden Memories

How is your mini-garden growing now? What does it look like? Draw it.

How about saving a leaf from your mini-garden so you can always remember it? Dry it and place it here.

Chapter 6
A Friendly Message for Future Daisies

Day after day, week after week, the girls visited the garden. They planted herbs and watered all the seedlings that sprouted. They tended their worm composting boxes, hatched their ladybugs, and delivered fresh compost to the garden. All the while they talked with Amazing Daisy and her flower friends. They got to know each flower, one by one.

One sunny afternoon, Chandra was watering the flowers with her shiny silver watering can. "You know," she said, "each of you flower friends has a place in our Girl Scout Law.

"Lupe, you are honest and fair. Sunny, you are friendly and helpful. Zinni, you are considerate and caring."

"And Tula," said Cora, "you are courageous and strong. Mari, you are responsible for what you say and do. And you, Gloria, respect yourself and others."

"And, Gerri, you respect authority," said Campbell. "Clover, you use resources wisely. And, Rosie, you make the world a better place."

"And Vi," all three girls sang out together, "you remind us to be a sister to every Girl Scout."

"This has been the best-ever way to learn the Girl Scout Law," said Campbell. "I can say the whole Law by heart just by thinking about Lupe and Sunny and Zinni . . ."

"And Tula and Mari and Gloria . . ."

"And Gerri and Clover and Rosie . . ."

"And Vi," all three girls sang out together.

"I was so glad that Mrs. Flores let all three of us say the Law together at our Girl Scout meeting yesterday," said Cora. "That was so much fun. I think all the other Girl Scout Daisies were surprised that we could say it so fast."

"And explain it, too," said Chandra. "We really have something to celebrate now. Let's invite all the Girl Scout Daisies to our garden party."

"Let's invite our neighbors, too," said Campbell.

"Let's invite the whole town," said Cora. "This garden belongs to everybody. Everybody should meet Amazing Daisy and all her flower friends. And everybody can learn about planting and growing . . ."

"And ladybugs and worm composting," Chandra said with a laugh.

"What do you think, Amazing Daisy?" Campbell asked.

"Well, I love a good garden party," Daisy said. "And party food is always so pretty."

"And it smells good, too," Gerri added.

Let's Throw a Party!

What would you serve at your garden party? Who would you invite?

Draw a picture of your party.

"So now," said Daisy, "you girls have just one more thing to do."

"That's right," said Rosie. "You are going to write a special message for next year's Girl Scout Daisies, just like Daisy Gordon Low wrote to you."

"We know! We know! We know!" the three girls sang out.

"We've been thinking about it a long time," said Cora. "Are you ready, BFFs?"

Cora pulled out a pencil and paper and began to write:

84

Dear New Girl Scout Daisies:

In your first year as Girl Scouts, you will do many wonderful things. One of them is to get to know the Girl Scout Law. It might seem hard at first. You might have trouble remembering all the lines. But soon you will see that the Law is written in a special way. Each line comes in its proper order. The early lines really do need to come early. Like, "I will do my best to be honest and fair, friendly and helpful, considerate and caring." Those are the early lines of the Law, because you really need to be all those things before you can be anything else.

$\longrightarrow$

That's what we learned in this garden full of flower friends. Without Amazing Daisy, we would not have met all the flowers. And all the flowers helped us learn each line of the Girl Scout Law. So enjoy your time as Girl Scout Daisies. Be honest and fair, and friendly and helpful, and considerate and caring whenever you can. And be courageous and strong, and responsible. Remember to respect yourself and others, and respect authority. And be sure to use resources wisely. And be a sister to every Girl Scout. If you are all these things, you can do many great things. Most of all, you can make the world a better place.

Cora   Campbell   Chandra

What do you want to tell next year's new Girl Scout Daisies?